# Dear David

*A Mother's Letters to Heaven*

*Carrie Wardencki-Currier*

# Dedication

*I dedicate this book to my three children: David, Jace, and Kaydence. If given the chance, I would choose you all over again. Love, Mom.*

| David, age 15 | Kaydence age 13 | Jace age 15 |

# Acknowledgments

*A very special thank you*
*To my loving husband, Jonathan Currier: You are my rock,*
*my strength when I am weak, and my solid ground when life*
*gets shaky. I could not have done this without you. Olive*
*juice.*

# 17 Famous Quotes about Death

1. *When someone you love becomes a memory,*
   *the memory becomes a treasure.*

   *Author unknown*

2. *Tears are the silent language of grief.*

   *Voltaire*

3. *Grief is the price we pay for love.*

   *Queen Elizabeth II*

4. *Grief changes shape but never ends.*

   *Keanu Reeves*

5. *The life of the dead is placed in the memory of the living,*
   *Marcus.*

   *Tullius Cicero*

6. *Give sorrow words; the grief that does not speak*
   *whispers the o'er-fraught heart and bids it break.*

   *William Shakespeare*

7. *Why does it take a minute to say hello*
   *and forever to say goodbye?*

   *Author unknown*

8. *I don't know why they call it heartbreak.*
   *It feels like every part of my body is broken, too.*

   *Chloe Woodward*

9. *We get no choice: if we love, we grieve.*

   *Thomas Lynch*

10. Death is a part of all of our lives; whether we like it or
    not, it is bound to happen. Instead of avoiding thinking
    about it, it is better to understand its meaning.

    **Dalai Lama**

11. If we live, we live for the Lord; and if we die, we die for
    the Lord. So whether we live or die, we belong to the
    Lord.

    **Romans 14:8**

12. Our dead are never dead to us until we have forgotten
    them.

    **George Eliot**

13. If tears could build a stairway and memories a lane,
    I'd walk right up to heaven and bring you home again.

    **Author unknown**

14. Memory is a way of holding on to the things you love,
    the things you are, and the things you would never want to
    lose.

    **Fred Savage** *(from The Wonder Years)*

15. Grief can't be shared. Everyone carries it alone,
    his own burden in his own way.

    **Anne Morrow Lindbergh**

16. Her absence is like the sky, spread over everything.

    **C.S. Lewis**

17. Your death has forever changed me.

    **Carrie Wardencki-Currier**

# Introduction

Dear Reader,

David was born on November 8th, 2003. He was my firstborn son, and he was everything to me. He came into this world after our family suffered the tragic death of his uncle David, whom he was named after. He was a radiant light that gave us all hope and brought joy to so many people. My heart aches for him every day. I want my joy back.

David's death came quickly and unexpectedly, as most young people's do. I never got to say goodbye. The how and the why of his untimely death are not relevant—he is gone and never coming back. He was taken from this world on February 5th, 2021, a day I will never forget. Every day since, I've been living in a fog, just existing. This is a wound that does not heal. His death is now part of me, as David was, is, and always will be.

When I started writing these letters to my son, my intention was for them to stay private between David and me. After reluctantly sharing one in a grief group and seeing how it inspired others to write letters to their lost loved ones, I decided to put them together in this book.

David was 17 years old when he died, so I carefully chose 17 letters, hoping they will connect on a personal level with other parents who are unfortunately suffering in the same dreadful way. I chose letters that portray my grief—the way it changes and also, very much, stays the same.

I am not an author or a therapist, just a grieving parent like you. These letters are raw and real, all written in the throes of grief. My hope is that you will find some comfort in knowing you are not alone. We are not alone. I encourage you to use the empty pages at the back of this book to write to your loved ones in heaven too.

# *Letter 1*

*Dear David,*

*To my sweet, loving boy, I miss you so much. You're on my mind every minute of every day. You were taken too soon, and it doesn't seem fair. I don't know how to go on without you; some days, it seems impossible. My heart is so broken. I'll never see your radiant smile or hear your contagious laugh, or hear a simple "I love you, Mom," again. And I'll never be able to say "I love you" back—not here on Earth, anyway. It's painful—the worst pain I've ever experienced in my life.*

*I'm sorry I couldn't protect you from this tragedy. You deserved more—a better, longer life. There's so much more you should have gotten to experience, and now you'll never have the chance. I'm not ready to let you go, but I guess you were never really mine to keep. I wish we had more time as mother and son.*

*I love you, David Andrew Christopher. You will live on in my heart until we meet again in paradise.*

*I miss you.*

*I love you.*

*Love, Mom*

# Letter 2

Dear David,

I miss you—your laugh, your smile, and your kind heart. It's been a little over a month since you died, and I feel like everyone has moved on. I hate that—for you and for me. I want to cry, but the tears won't come. I know if I break down, that means all of this is real.

I'm looking at a picture of you when you were maybe a year and a half. I'd give anything to go back to that time and hold you tighter and longer. I regret every missed hug.

I miss you.

I love you.

Love, Mom

# *Letter 3*

*Dear David,*

*Each day that passes is a small step further away from the last time I saw you. I hate it. No one gets it. Sometimes I just want to scream to let people know I am still here, grieving you. You are still gone, and it will always hurt. People seem to have moved on, and I am still stuck in a loop on February 5th, 2021, at 10:23.*

*People say stupid things like, "He's in a better place," or "Be grateful for the 17 years you had," or my personal favorite: "You seem to be doing so well. I would never be able to carry on if I lost a child. How do you do it?" I want to throttle these people. Instead, I think of you and use it as a teaching moment. There should be a list of things not to say to a grieving mother.*

*None of this matters, though, because at the end of each thoughtless comment, you are still gone and never coming back.*

*I wish you were here.*

*I miss you.*

*I love you.*

*Love, Mom*

# Letter 4

Dear David,

I miss you terribly. None of this feels real. Am I ridiculous for writing to you? I don't even know what to say today. I just miss you so much.

I spend a lot of my days wondering what you'd be doing in life if you were still here. Also, would you be on my mind as much if you were still here, or would I be taking all the little moments for granted, as we all tend to do?

I want to go back and change so much. You were too good for this world, I guess. I have to tell myself this, because otherwise, there is the burning question: Why would God have taken a 17-year-old with so much promise and lust for life? My 17-year-old, who could have accomplished so many things.

I don't know the answers to any of this. I am just left with all the questions.

I miss you.

I love you.

Love, Mom

# *Letter 5*

*Dear David,*

*Yesterday was Mother's Day—just another day without you. I actually felt numb the entire day. I know I have your brother and sister to think about, but it's hard sometimes. Most of the time, I pretend you're still alive. It's easier this way.*

*I am scared that if I really feel all of my emotions about you being gone, I won't make it. I am angry all the time. It's my safe emotion because I don't want to find out where sad will lead. I'm angry that you weren't given a real shot, angry with myself, angry with God, angry with parents of living children, and angry that I feel angry all the time. None of this feels real.*

*I know one day it's all going to come crashing down on me like a pile of very heavy, overwhelming, sad bricks, and I don't know what I'm going to do with the emotions when that day comes. In all honesty, I'm scared for that day.*

*I'll probably continue to mask my emotions for now. It's the only way I know how to deal with your death. It might not be the right way, but it's my way for today.*

*I miss you.*

*I love you.*

*Love, Mom*

# Letter 6

*Dear David,*

*Today is a really rough day—as if all of them aren't rough. My insides feel turned upside down, and my world is in silent chaos. I keep you and your death hidden away sometimes. Not because I don't want to talk about you to the world—I do—but because I don't want to talk about your death to the world.*

*When people hear that I have lost a child (I hate that terminology; I didn't lose you in a grocery store—you died), that's all they want to talk about. They want to know the specifics, but it's not their business. And what does it matter? At the end of the day, you're still gone, and they get to walk away from the conversation, go buy a gallon of milk, or put gas in their car. I'm left emptier than when I started.*

*When am I going to wake up from this nightmare? I still expect you to walk through the front door. I still expect to hear your voice. Oh, how I miss your voice.*

*I wish we could trade places. Given the opportunity, I would.*

*I miss you.*

*I love you.*

*Love, Mom*

# *Letter 7*

Dear David,

Today marks two years since you have been gone. I am still so broken. I force a fake smile and keep going, but all the while, I'm dying on the inside. It's easier for me to pretend that you are safe somewhere, living a happy life.

Nobody really understands this pain unless they've suffered the kind of loss I'm suffering now. My heart breaks with and for them. I want to scream and break things so my pain can be seen and heard—so people can see something other than my forced smile. Everyone seems to have moved on. Not me. I will never move on from this.

Each day takes me further away from the day you died, but I hold you close to my heart and soul. I honored your memory again this year by donating to the ice fishing tournament—the second-place winner, of course. I know you would want it that way. You were so kind like that.

I will go through the motions today, visiting your grave and wishing I could turn back the hands of time to February 4th, 2021, to save you from the untimely death that would come the very next day.

I live on every day for your brother and sister. They need me; they're hurting too. I have to stay here for them, for now.

I miss you.

I love you.

Love, Mom

# Letter 8

Dear David,

My eyes burn from all the tears. I have so many thoughts and unanswered questions. Where would you be? What would you be doing?

I miss you so much. There's an enormous hole in my heart that will never be filled. You're missing everything, and it's absolutely unfair. Every day feels the same as the last, and nothing in the world feels right.

You will forever be in my heart.

I miss you.

I love you.

Love, Mom

# *Letter 9*

*Dear David,*

*It's 3:23 in the morning. Sleep is so difficult most nights or just flat-out nonexistent. I'm sitting here, thinking about every moment I won't get to spend with you.*

*The past couple of weeks have been rough—realizing I'll never have a new picture to look at, a text to read, or a voicemail to listen to. This is hitting me hard. I get a little piece of you through watching your brother grow up. He looks more and more like you, but he talks about you less and less. It's killing me.*

*I feel like I'm the only one still deeply affected by your death, though I know that's not true. I know your brother still misses you; he just has his own way of dealing with it. Your sister is grieving too, in her own way. I just wish we said your name more—shared more stories.*

*I know they have to live their lives. Your death can't be theirs too. It can't be all-encompassing, like it is for me.*

*I miss you.*

*I love you.*

*Love, Mom*

*Side by Side of Jace, left (14-years-old) & David, right (15-years-old)*

# *Letter 10*

Dear David,

Twenty years ago today, you were safely tucked away in my belly while your father and I committed ourselves to each other before God, family, and friends. We were so young. I truly believed in that moment, on that day, when I said, "I do," that it would be forever.

Little did we know that just two short months later, your father's brother, David—whom you were named after—would pass away. His death set off a chain of events that would eventually lead to yours 17 years later.

Today, I sit here and think about all the "what ifs." What if your uncle had never died—would you still be here? What if I had run away from all the chaos and started a new life, just you and me? Would you have had more time—the time you so deserved— to live your precious life.

As I write this, I'm looking at your picture, as I often do when writing to you. I wonder, am I wasting my time? Do you hear me when I read these letters at your graveside? Or is this all in vain?

I don't know, my blue-eyed, beautiful boy. What I do know is that I will love you until my last breath. I loved you before you took your first breath, and that love will never die—it can never die— even though you did.

I miss you.

I love you.

Love, Mom

# Letter 11

*Dear David,*

*It has been eight months since you died. Today, I found a carving on the basement wall that you must have made before you passed. I've been in that basement almost every day, to do laundry, and never once noticed it until now. It says, clear as day, "DAVID WAS HERE"*

*And yes, you were, my beautiful son. You were here, and you left such a big imprint on so many people's lives. I got this exact carving tattooed on my arm in your memory.*

*I often ask for signs from you, and I guess this was one of the biggest signs I could have received. It's still not enough, though. It did, however, bring me some solace in that moment, so thank you for that. Still, I selfishly want more.*

*Death is such a natural part of life, but it feels so unnatural for a parent to lose a child. I'll never understand why this happened—to you, to me, to our family.*

*I miss you.*

*I love you.*

*Love, Mom*

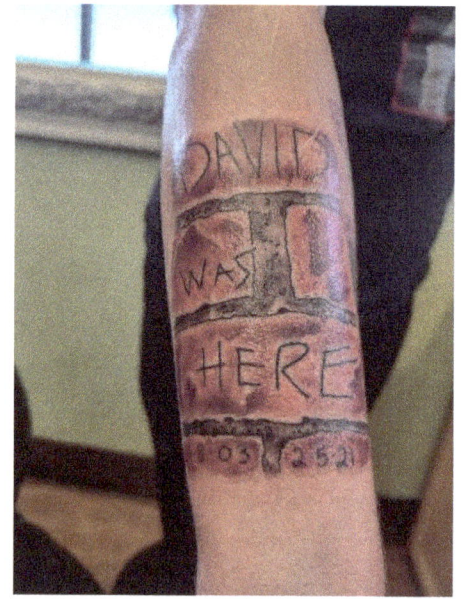

# Letter 12

Dear David,

Jace, Kaydence, and I went to your grave today. I hate seeing your name inscribed on that footstone. Sometimes, I feel like I could stay there for hours, talking to you, and other times, I feel like you're not there at all—that you're everywhere instead.

All of this still feels so foreign to me. I don't think it will ever become normal. People say, "your new normal," but I can't seem to accept that. I guess it's the reality of the situation, but I'm not ready to face it—not yet.

How does someone so young, bright, vibrant, amazing, handsome, loving, caring, kind, and beautiful become a pile of ashes buried in the ground? When will I wake up from this nightmare? It's a question I find myself asking over and over again to anyone who will listen.

I miss you.

I love you.

Love, Mom

# *Letter 13*

*Dear David,*

*It has been 9 months, 41 weeks, 189 days, 6,942 hours, and 416,520 minutes since you died—almost the same amount of time I carried you in my belly before you made your debut into this world. I can promise you that both of these events feel like they just happened yesterday.*

*A lot has been going on since your journey home to God. None of it feels real or right without you here, though. I vividly remember the day I gave birth to you—I never knew I could love someone so much. That day changed my life forever, in such a beautiful way.*

*I wish we had more months, weeks, days, hours, and minutes together. I wasn't ready for you to go.*

*I miss you.*

*I love you.*

*Love, Mom*

# *Letter 14*

*Dear David,*

*I miss you so much it hurts. I can't understand why the world didn't stop when you died. You are so very loved and missed. All of this is so unfair.*

*Come visit me in my dreams tonight.*

*I miss you.*

*I love you.*

*Love, Mom*

# *Letter 15*

Dear David,

Tonight is another late, restless night. I cannot get the image of you lying in that coffin out of my head. I keep thinking about your cold, stiff hands, your lifeless body—how you looked nothing like yourself. This is not how I want to remember you, but it's an image that often comes into my mind.

I feel as if everything flew by—the planning of your funeral, deciding what pictures to use, what songs to play, the coffin you would be viewed in, and what urn would hold your remains. These are decisions no parent should ever have to make. So many of your friends were there—the entire Funeral Home was packed. I'm sure you saw from wherever you are. You were a bright star that died out before your time—or maybe it was exactly your time. I just wasn't ready.

I hear that everyone has a purpose here on Earth, and as much as it hurts, I guess you served yours. It doesn't make it any easier, though. I don't even feel right writing that. This pain is just so unbearable.

I miss you.

I love you.

Love, Mom

# *Letter 16*

*Dear David,*

*I had another sleepless night. I'm so tired of pretending everything is OK and putting a smile on my face for everyone. Someone told me I look so put together, not like someone who has just lost a child. How am I supposed to look? I don't have a choice but to go on. I mean, I guess I do. I could end everything, but where would that leave your brother and sister—without a brother and a mother? I won't do that to them. I can't do that to them, as much as I want to be with you.*

*Sometimes I picture you in heaven, in all your glory, with huge oceans, lakes, rivers, and ponds to fish in—stocked fresh every day for you. I loved your passion for fishing, and I loved your patience when you were teaching me how to do what you loved most. These are memories I'll cherish forever.*

*Save me a pole and the seat next to you. We will fish again together one day.*

*I miss you.*

*I love you.*

*Love, Mom*

*David (16-years-old) with his big catch.*

# *Letter 17*

Dear David,

We are swiftly approaching the fourth anniversary of your death. It still feels like yesterday. The pain is still very real, raw, and tender. My grief has definitely grown, or I have grown with my grief—however you want to look at it. I still hold you so close in my heart with everything that I do.

I am now able to look back on some memories and smile, instead of being angry all the time or breaking down in tears. The anger and sadness are still there, though—it's just not all day, every day. I will still never understand why you were taken from me. I'll never come to terms with it.

Your death was tragic, but your life was beautiful, as were you. Talking about you in the past tense is still so difficult. I know that your soul will live on forever. It is just your body we can no longer see.

Thank you for choosing me to be your mother. I will love you now, always, and forever, until we meet again.

I miss you.

I love you.

Love, Mom

*Me and David; our very last picture together*

*Me and David goofing around.*

*David (8-years-old) doing what he loves—fishing!*

| David 14-years-old | David 6-years-old | Kay, Jace, & David |

*In loving memory of David Andrew Christopher Wardencki*
*11/08/03 to 02/05/2021 GONE BUT NEVER FORGOTTEN* ♥ 🖤 ♥ 🖤

*Dear*_____

_____

_____

_____

_____

_____

_____

_____

_____

_____

_____

_____

_____

_____

_____

_____

_____

_____

_____

_____

_____

_____

_____

_____

_____

_____

*Dear*_____

_____

_____

_____

_____

_____

_____

_____

_____

_____

_____

_____

_____

_____

_____

_____

_____

_____

_____

_____

_____

_____

*Dear*_____

_____

_____

_____

_____

_____

_____

_____

_____

_____

_____

_____

_____

_____

_____

_____

_____

_____

_____

_____

_____

_____

_____

*Dear*_____

_____

_____

_____

_____

_____

_____

_____

_____

_____

_____

_____

_____

_____

_____

_____

_____

_____

_____

_____

_____

Dear_____

_____

_____

_____

_____

_____

_____

_____

_____

_____

_____

_____

_____

_____

_____

_____

_____

_____

_____

_____

_____

_____

_____

*Dear*_____

_____

_____

_____

_____

_____

_____

_____

_____

_____

_____

_____

_____

_____

_____

_____

_____

_____

_____

_____

_____

Dear_____

*Dear*_____

*Dear*_____

_____

_____

_____

_____

_____

_____

_____

_____

_____

_____

_____

_____

_____

_____

_____

_____

_____

_____

_____

_____

_____

_____

_____

_____

*Dear*_____

_____

_____

_____

_____

_____

_____

_____

_____

_____

_____

_____

_____

_____

_____

_____

_____

_____

_____

_____

_____

*Dear*_____

_____

_____

_____

_____

_____

_____

_____

_____

_____

_____

_____

_____

_____

_____

_____

_____

_____

_____

_____

_____

_____

_____

_____

*Dear*_____

_____

_____

_____

_____

_____

_____

_____

_____

_____

_____

_____

_____

_____

_____

_____

_____

_____

_____

_____

_____

_____

_____

*Dear*_____

*Painting of David, artist credit Mal Holcomb-Botts*

www.ingramcontent.com/pod-product-compliance
Lightning Source LLC
Chambersburg PA
CBHW051249120626
46547CB00014B/1860